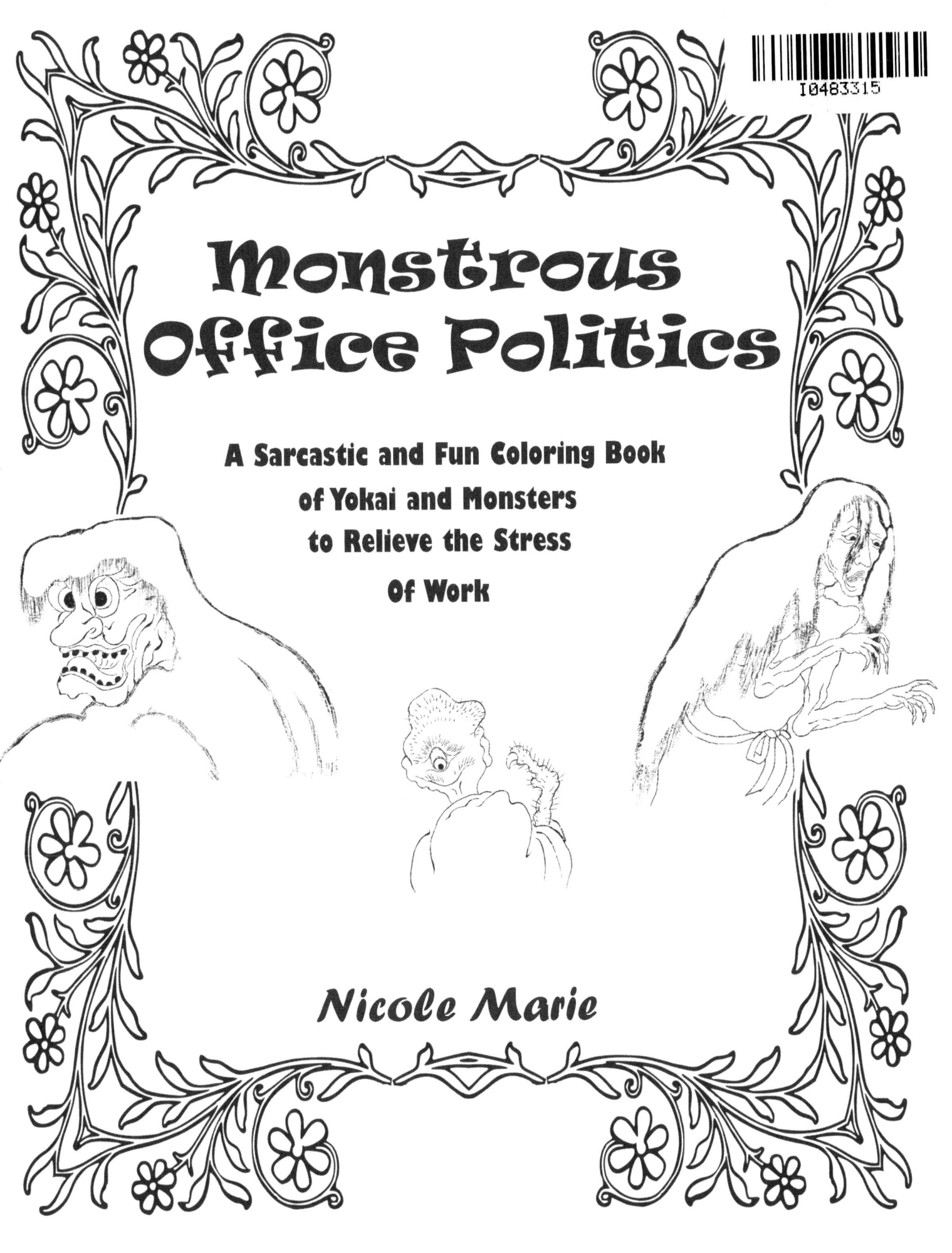

Monstrous Office Politics

A Sarcastic and Fun Coloring Book of Yokai and Monsters to Relieve the Stress Of Work

Nicole Marie

Dear Employee,

Incredibly fortunate people find jobs where they genuinely love their co-workers and have passion for the work that they do.

This book is not for those people or about those jobs.

This book is for those of us who exist somewhere between horrendous and tolerable at work.

Office politics are what happens when you bring random people, from all walks of life, with varying agendas, together to earn money. By wandering through office politics we learn what we are made of, what is important, who we value, and where our boundaries lye.

Over the years, I have had many different jobs, including teaching, real estate, social services, retail, and corporate. Sometimes co-workers were horribly monstrous to each other and other times we were all just a little shady.

You may wonder what monsters, folklore, and art have to do with offices and work.   The beauty of folklore is in the power of a story to communicate timeless universal truths about humans existing together. The power of art is a visual expression of the same.   Both folklore and art provide a safe place for us to gain insight and commiseration about any area of life, including work.

Japanese Yokai, in particular were the inspiration for this coloring book. Yokai are supernatural monsters or spirits that range in purpose and activity from extremely malevolent to silly and mischievous. Sometimes Yokai can also bring good fortune. Yokai are also the inspiration for popular games like Pokemon.¬¬

I have also included the work of two other artists focused on monsters. Fortunio Liceit's De Monstris, written in 1665, is an illustrated book about deformities in nature and most likely spear-headed the development of the circus freak show. Arent van Bolten was a Dutch artist who drew pictures of grotesque figures and monsters in the 17th century.   Each coloring page is preceded by the name of the Yokai or the artist's picture and a brief explanation of the coloring page.

The purpose of this coloring book is to have a cathartic, deviant, laugh at yourself and your co-workers.   It will, hopefully, be a humorous, stress relieving place for commiseration, and support for keeping it all in perspective. For some people, it may be best to only use this book outside of the office and avoid the risk of offending other people. Stay out of trouble, laugh out loud, color something beautiful, let it go, and be refreshed to face another day!

You Got This!

Happy Coloring!

Minokedachi

身の毛立

Minokedachi is an old, hunched over monster whose body hair is standing on end. Some believe that this monster haunts people and causes them to whine, complain, and gripe incessantly.

When I saw this monster, I immediately pictured several whin-ny, burnt out people who either need to quit their jobs or at least take a break.

The next time you see the grumpicus in your life, don't let the negativity bring you down. Just smile and imagine Minokedachi talking.

Color it out...

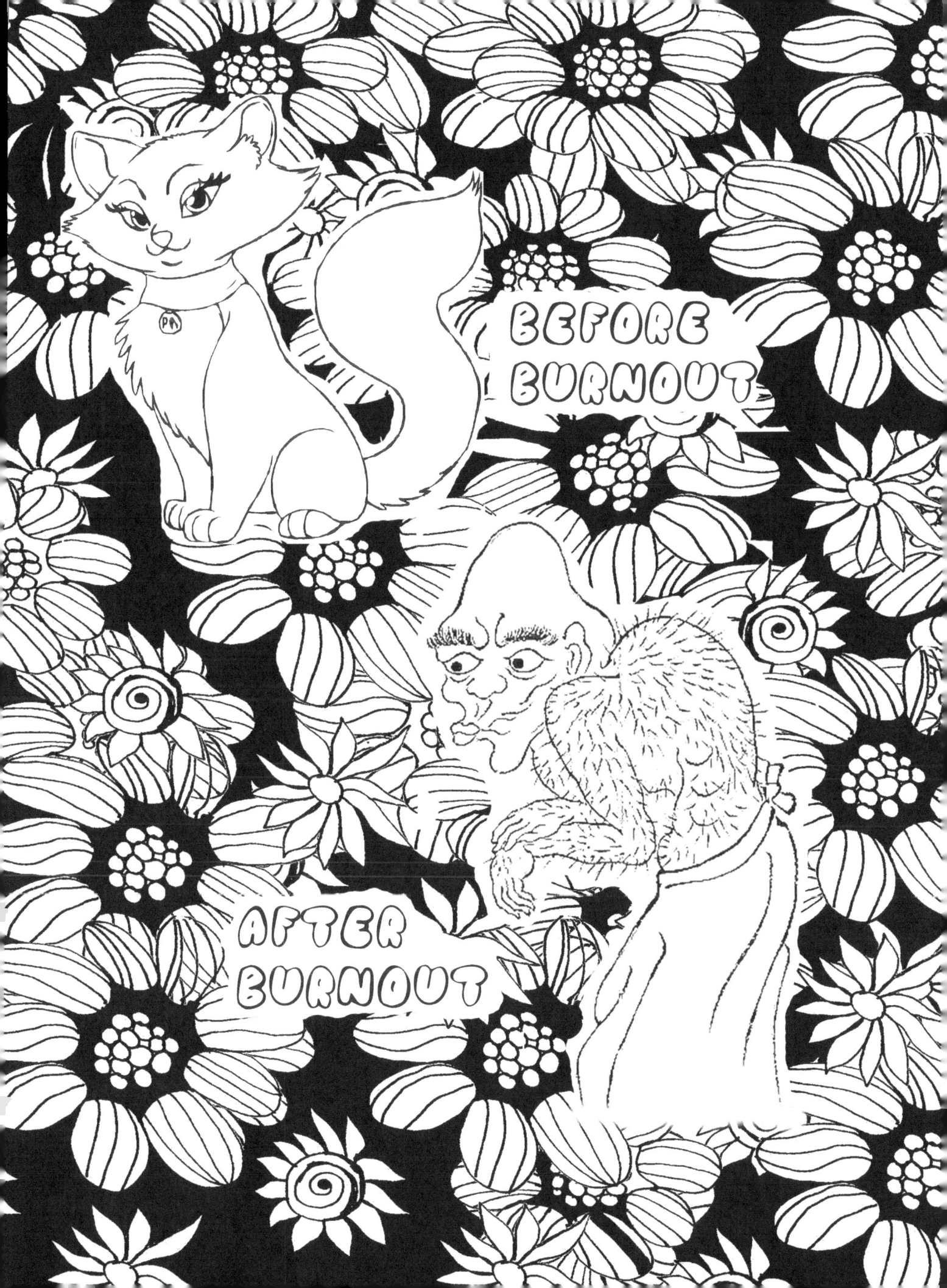

Nobusuma

のぶすま

Nobusuma means wild quilt. According to folklore the Nobusuma are bats that live to a very old age and then turn into magical bloodsucking monsters. This picture of a Nobusuma brought boredom and disinterest to my mind.

So, maybe the folklore doesn't fit with the picture I created or does it? I can definitely think of times when work felt like a dangerous bloodsucking bat that zapped away all of my enthusiasm.

Color it out....

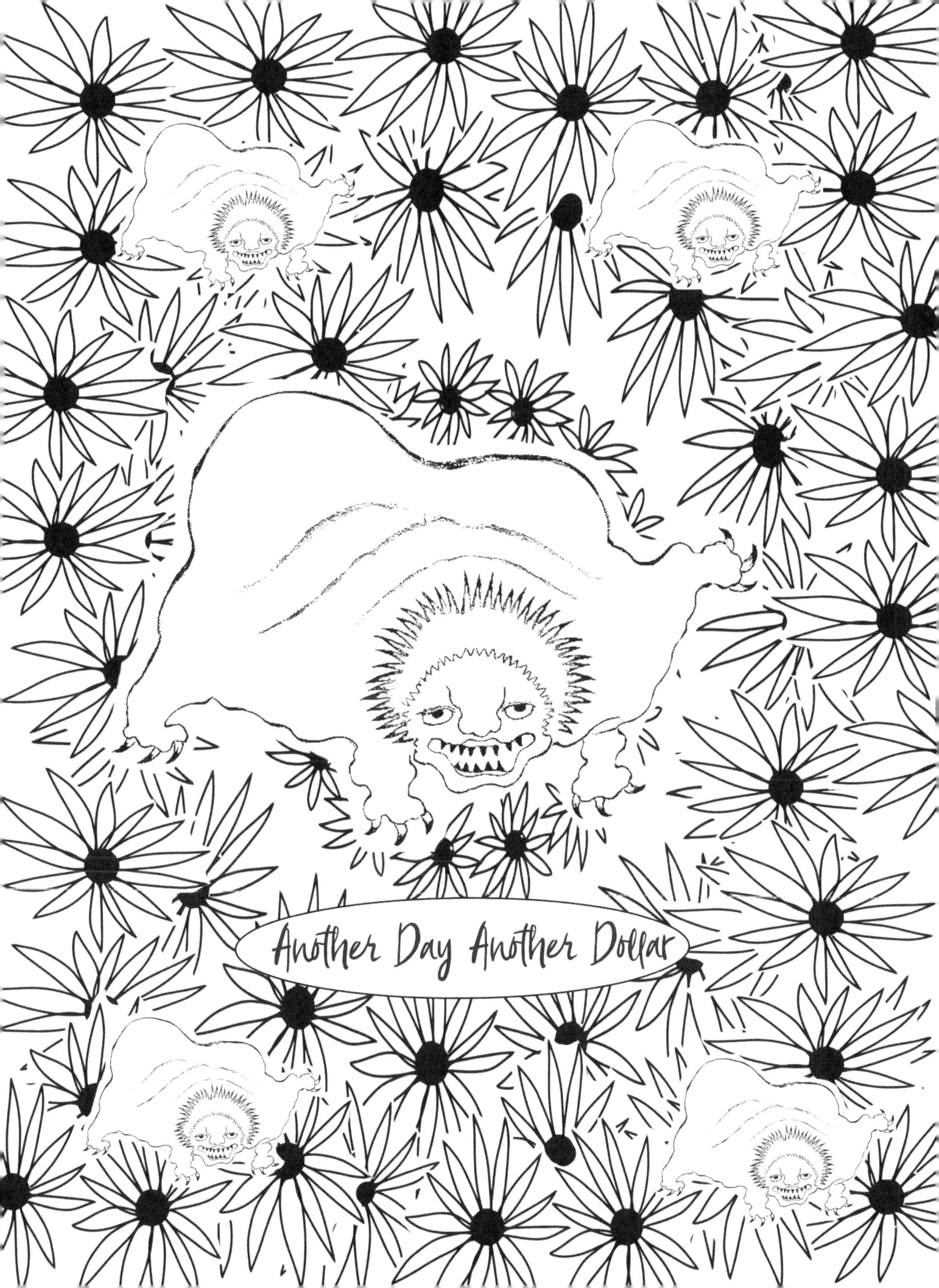

Twee Monsters Bereden Door Apen

Two Monsters Ride Through the Open

I am not sure what Arent van Bolten was thinking when he created this piece, but if just once I could have farted on my micromanager.

Color it out....

A gift for my

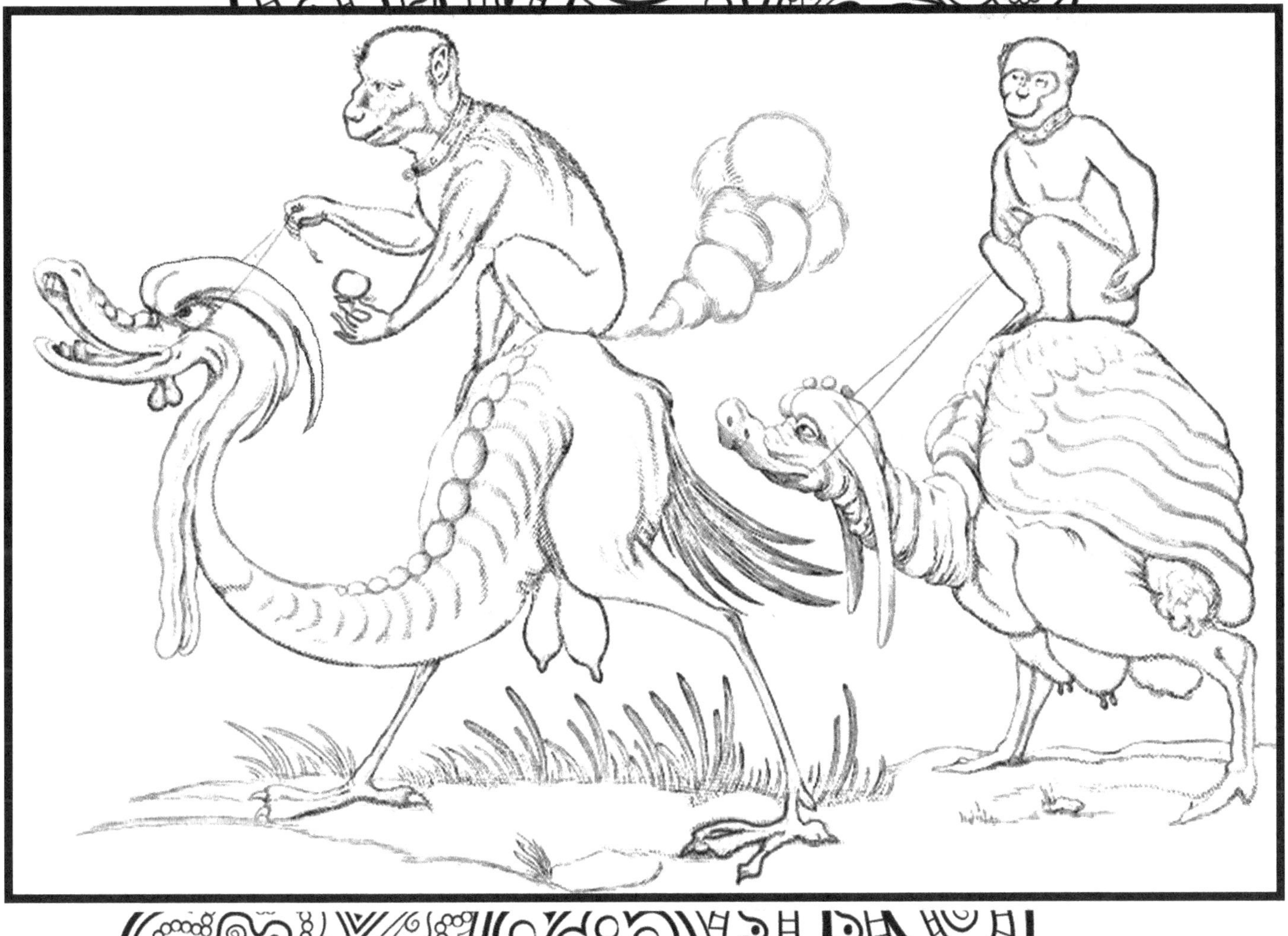

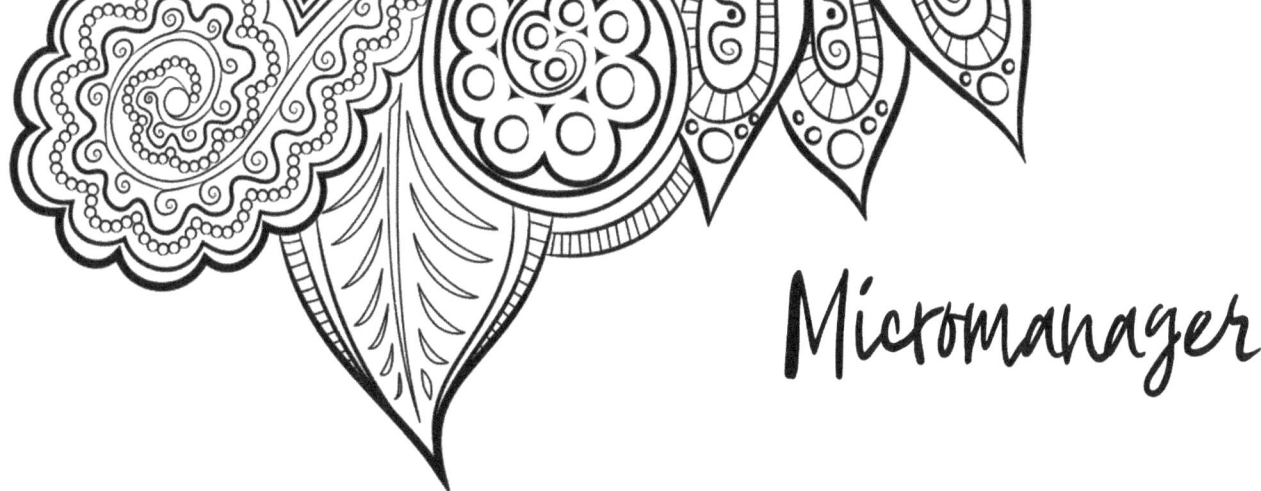

Micromanager

Buraribi & Hajikkaki

ぶらり火

はぢっかき

Buraribi is a flying monster surrounded by flames and it's name actually means aimless fire.

According to legend Buraribi are created from the souls of people who did not fully cross over into the next life after dying a physical death.

So, the folklore is a little morbid, but in the spirit of jest, I am sure that you can think of someone who rains down fire when he/she comes around.

When you are not running for cover, color and remember that burnt out people, burn up everyone around them. If you see yourself in this picture as Buraribi, please do everyone a favor.

Take a Break! Find a cooling happy place and color it out.

Unfortunately, I was not able to find much information about Hajikkaki, but this rendition of the spirit fit perfectly under Buraribi. I think it illustrates the duck and cover feeling well.

What do you think?

Color it out...

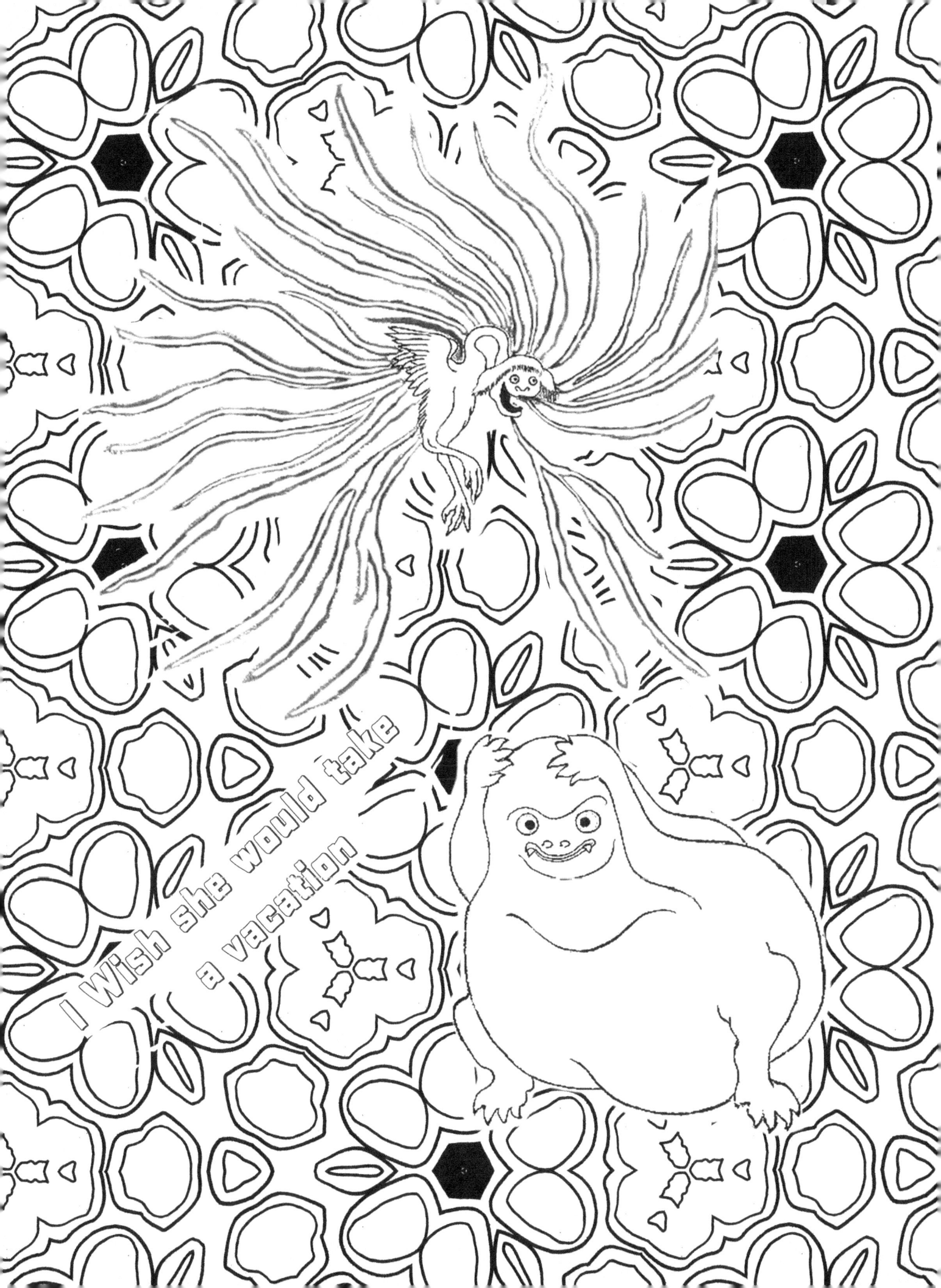

Domo-Komo

どうもこうも

Domo-Komo is a monster whose name carries the meaning "right and left." Actually, there is no official backstory for this fellow, but as far as work is concerned, I immediately thought of double-minded folks who talk a lot but, have little to say.

The next time you are in a meeting and someone who fits the bill starts to blab, picture Domo-Komo and have a good laugh.

Color it out....

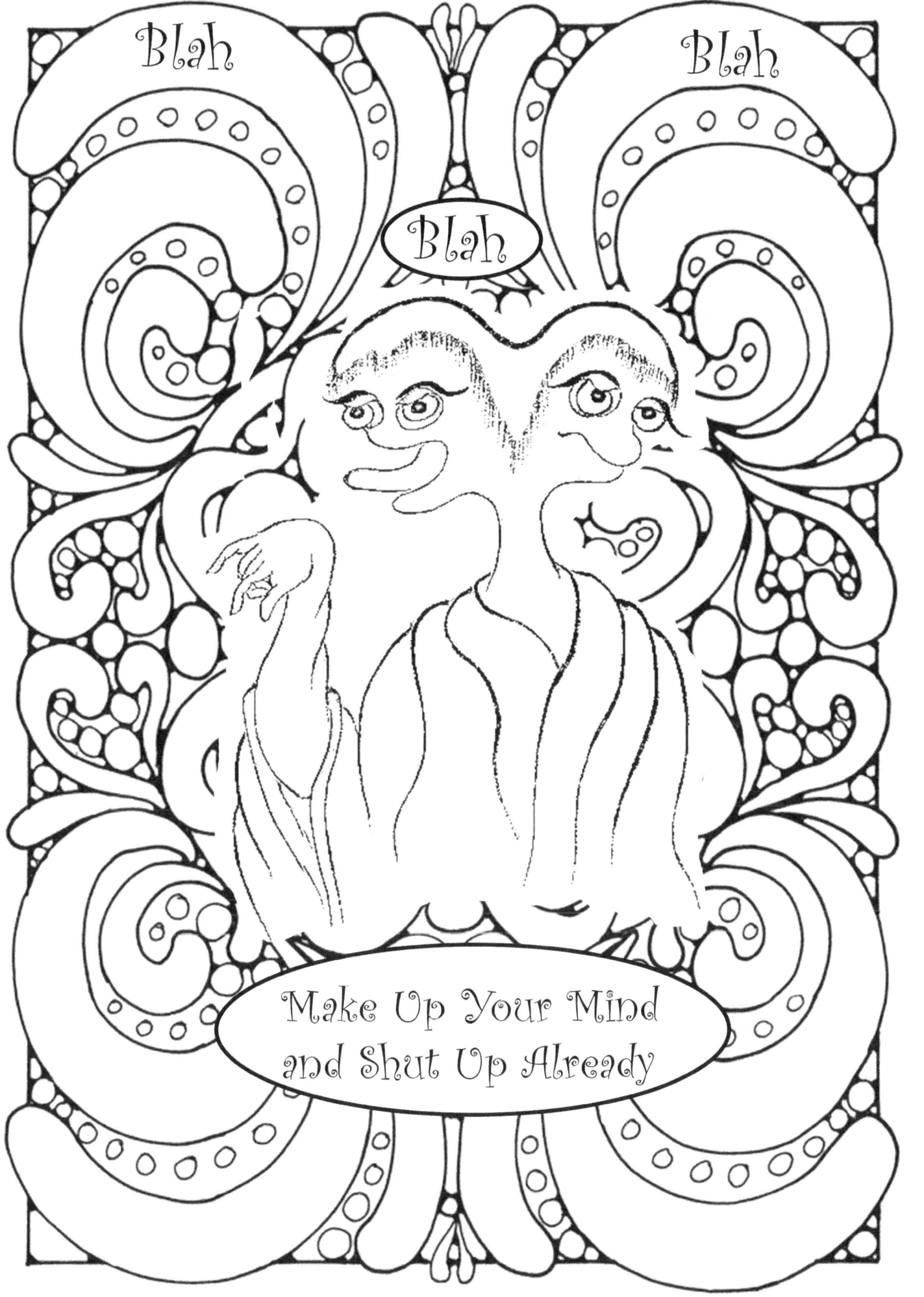

Twee Grotesken, Naar Links Lopend

Two Grotesques Walk to the Left

I think it is safe to assume that most workplaces have at least one of these characters.

If you are one of these characters, bullies are not sexy, please get over yourself, and start to practice random acts of kindness immediately.

If you know these characters smile when they are around and then ignore and avoid, ignore and avoid...

Smile and color it out....

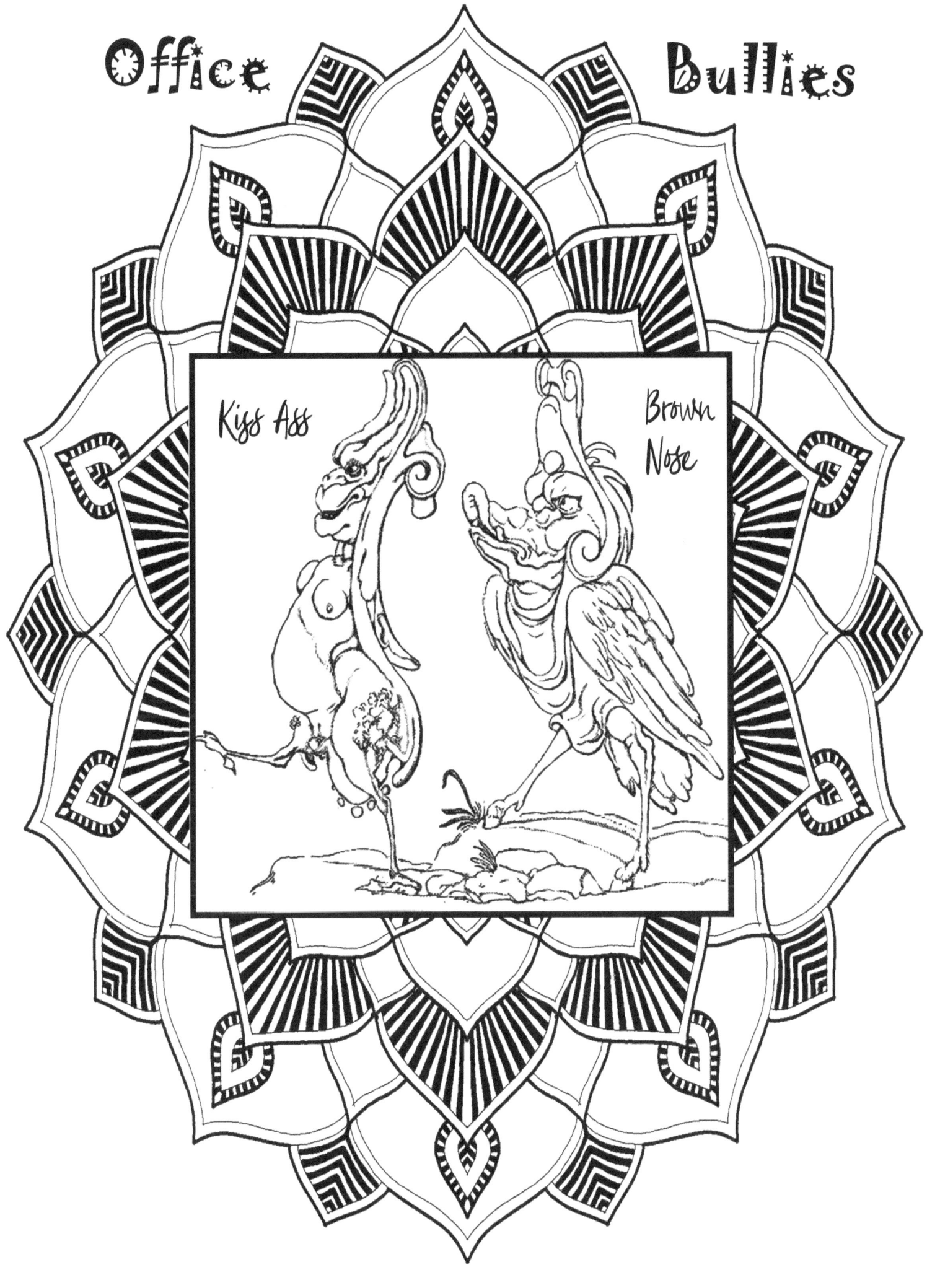

Fort lic de mon-
strorum caussis
Presentation of Monsterous Cases?

I do not read Latin, so I have no idea what Liceit was drawing but, how many of us have been completely overloaded with requirements, deliverables or task.

It's not possible for most of that stuff to get done anyway, so you might as well color instead.

Ok, maybe finish one task and then

Color it out...

By the way, Liceit was a bit freaky. He definately had a thing for nudity. In this picture you can also play "find the penis". Apparently, private parts are hidden all over the place in his work.

Perfect game with friends in a staff meeting!

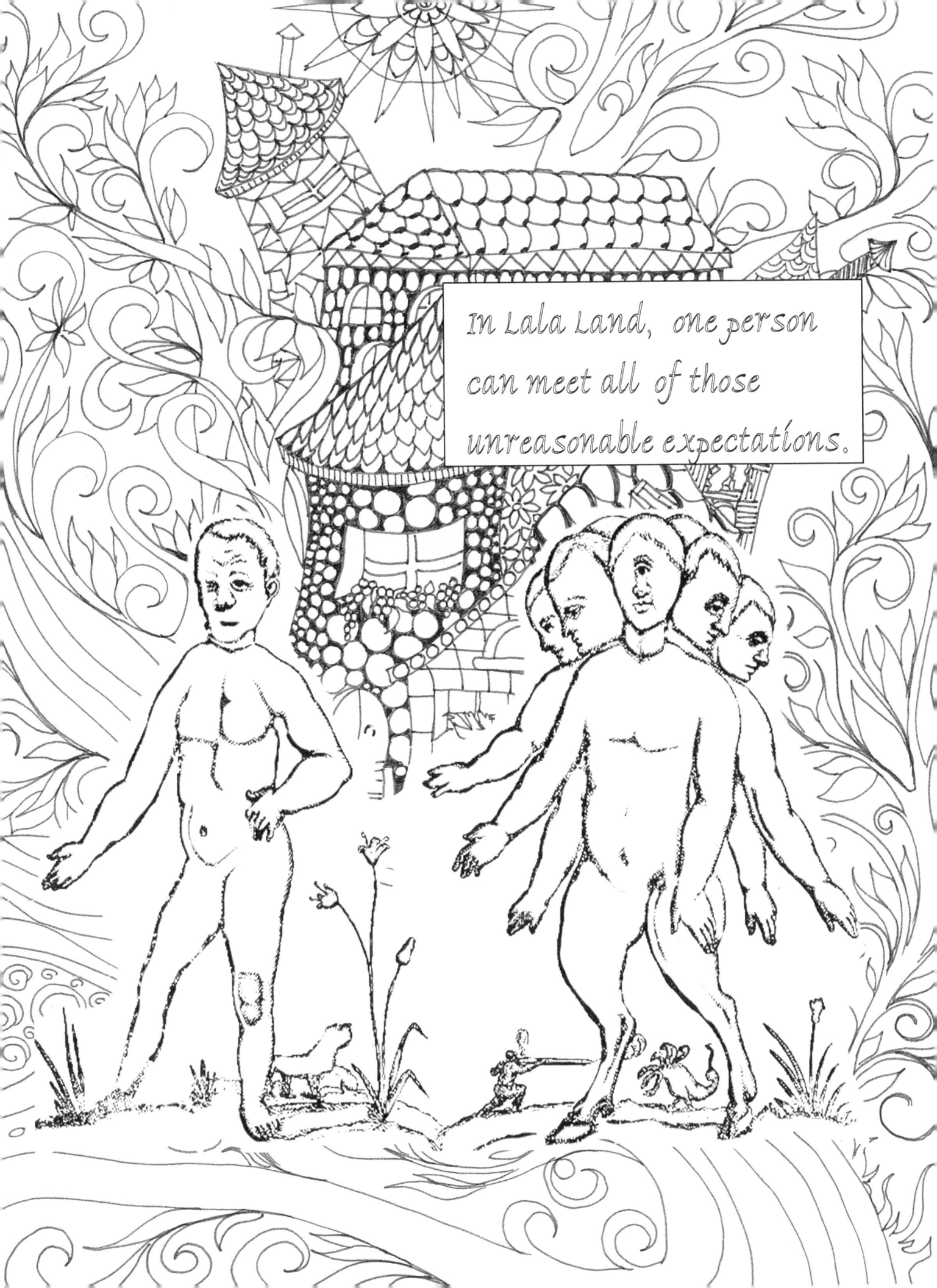

In Lala Land, one person can meet all of those unreasonable expectations.

Aka shita

赤舌

Aka shita means "red tongue". This monster is a dark cloud with sharp claws, a ghastly hairy face, and a long, bright, red tongue. Aka shita monsters bring bad luck and evil to those they visit.

Hopefully, when you sleep you dream of wonderful pleasures instead of stressful work stuff.

If work is causing nightmares, then hopefully you can color it out and leave it on the page.

Sweet Dreams.

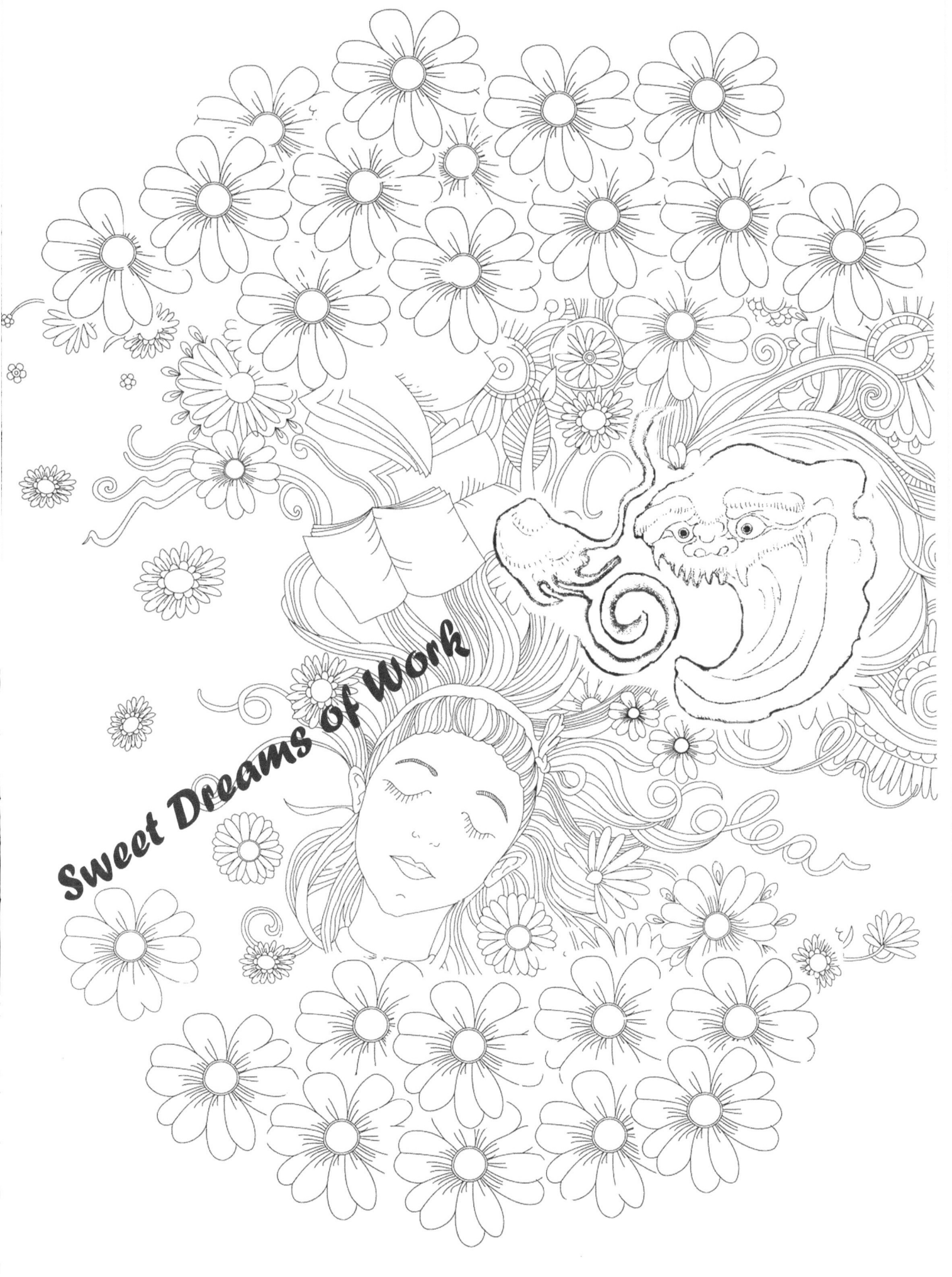

Sweet Dreams of Work

Mumashika

馬鹿

Mumashika literally means "horse deer" but the translated name of this Yokai is idiot or fool.

This comically, foolish fellow has the head of a one-eyed horse with a single horn in the back of the skull.

Some guess that this monster possesses people and causes them to behave foolishly.

Have you ever been on a committee when the choice of a lead has left you totally perplexed and smh?

Color it out....

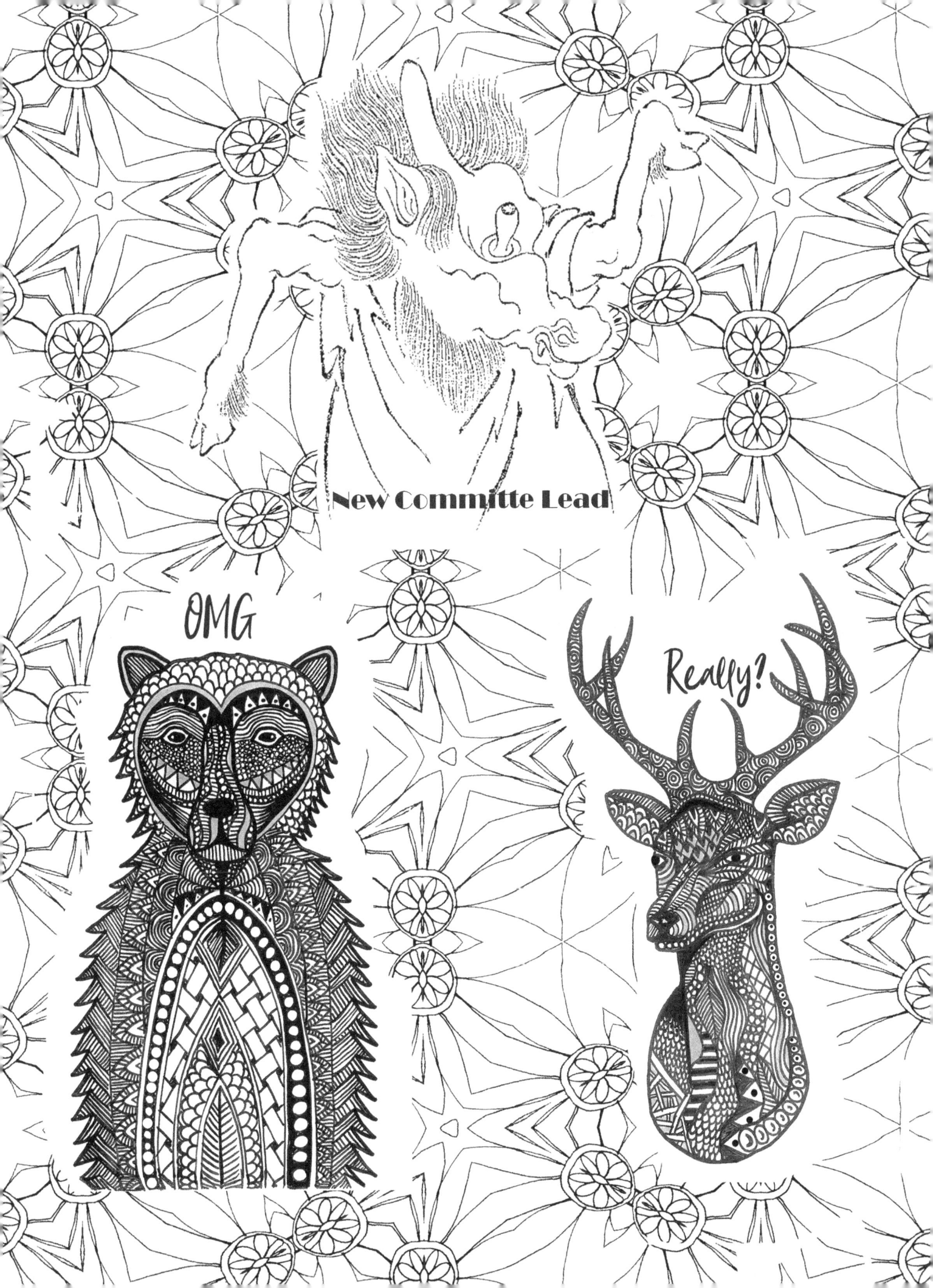

Rokurokubi
& Inugami

ろくろくび		犬神

Rokurokubi are female spirits who appear to be ordinary women during the day. At night, while they are asleep, their necks stretch and their heads roam freely. Becoming a Rokurokubi is a curse that a woman receives because of evil misdeeds that are often committed by her husband.

The other spirit in the picture is Inugami or dog spirit. Inugami are dog spirits that are the malicious remnants of abused dead dogs. Let's not repeat that to PETA.

As soon as I saw this picture I imagined this woman was telling this wicked dog spirit that he messed up an obviously simple, but important magical task by detaching her head.

Isn't it true, that when a simple but important task needs to be completed at work, that the most ridiculous mistakes are bound to happen!

Practice forgiveness and Color it Out...

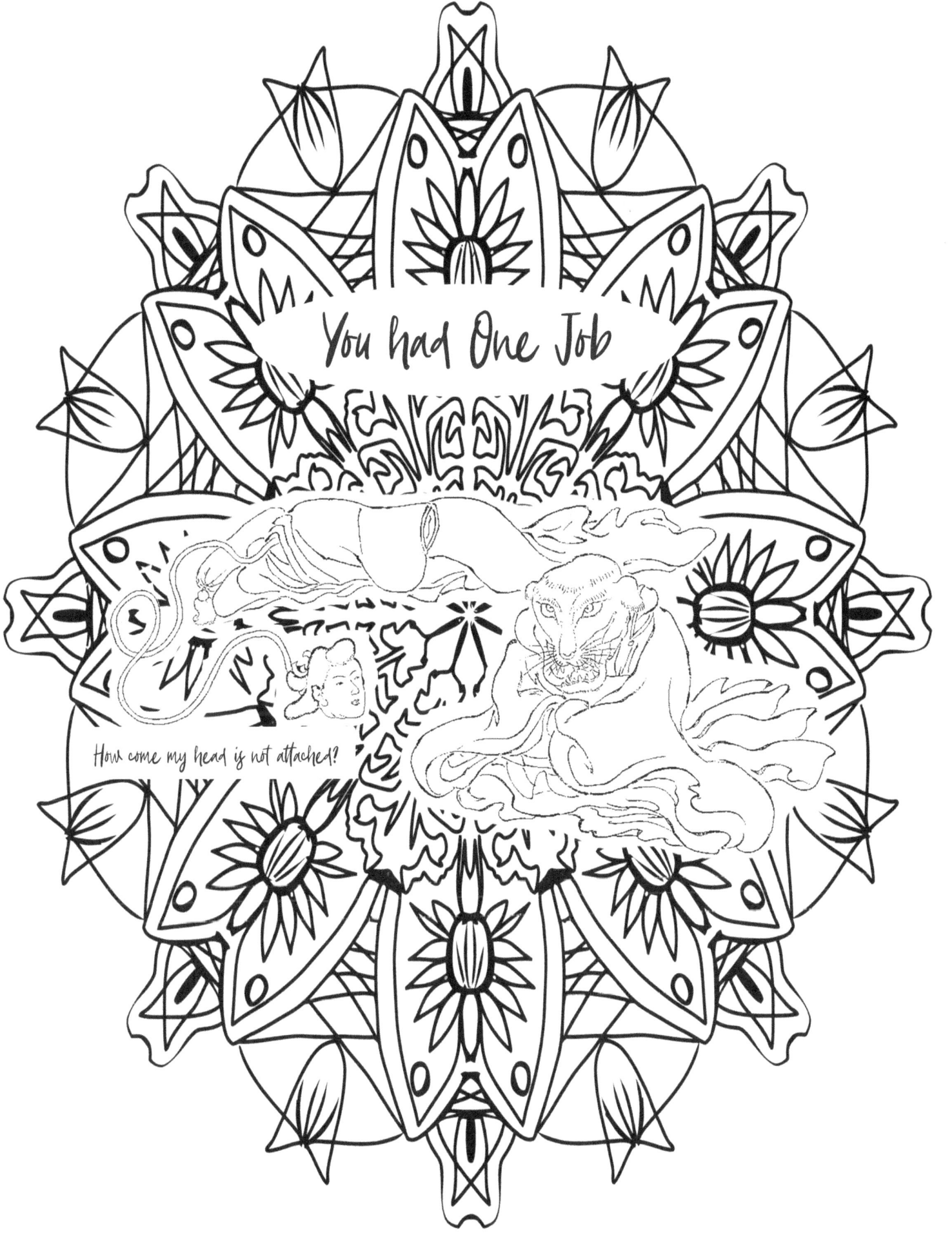

Oyajirome

親白眼

Oyajirome has a bulging eye in the back of its head. The folklore to go with this curvaceous, hooked handed monster is lost, but some believe that the eye in the back of the head means that no one can sneak up or hide things from it.

My thoughts are that if the eye is in the back of its head, how does the Oyajirome know where it is going? Does it travel backward or dwell in the past?

In any case, as far as work goes, it reminds me of people who have limited viewpoints or who spend hours looking everywhere but forward.

Color it out...

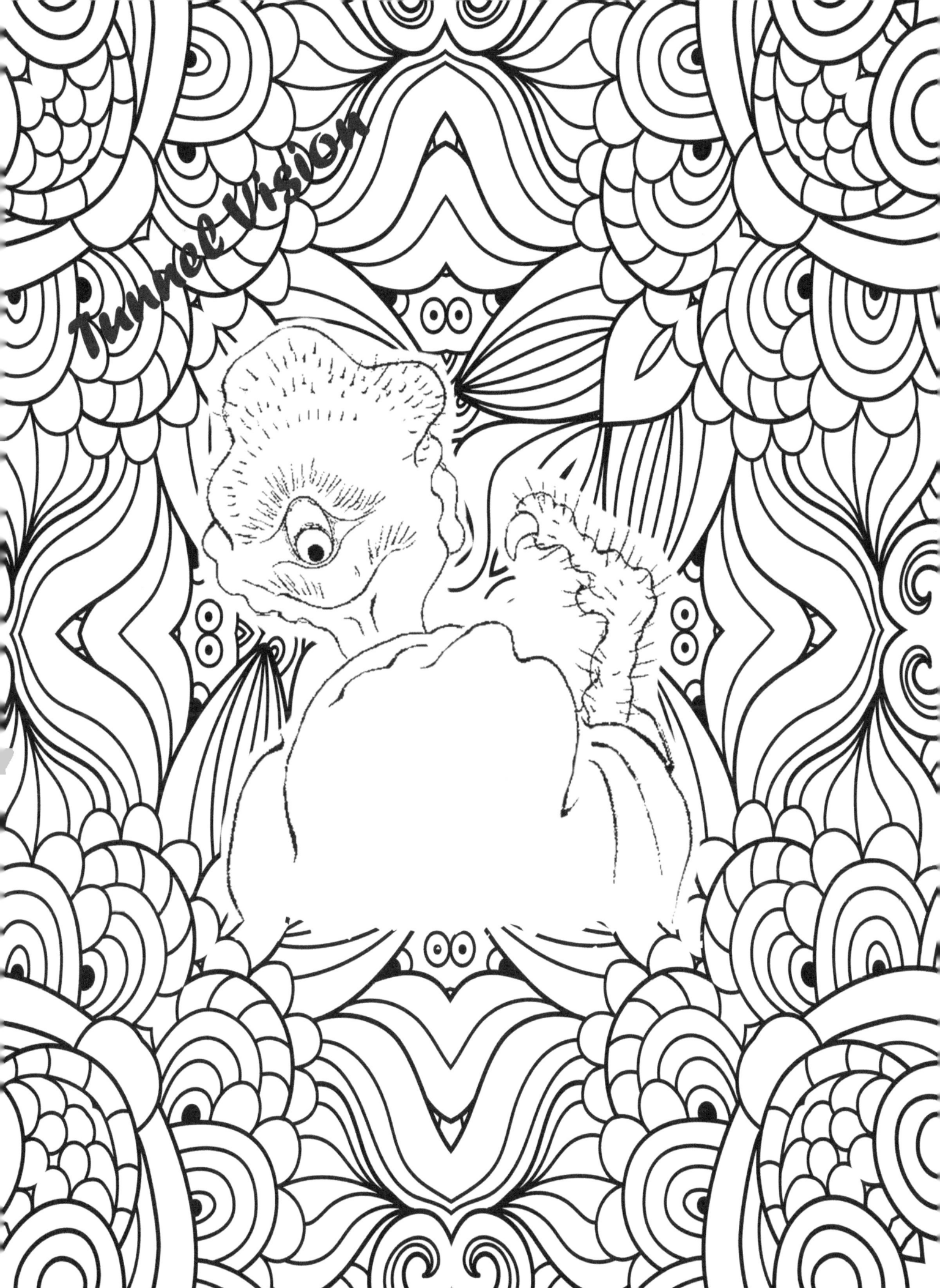

Fort lic de Monstrorum Caussis

Presentation of Monstrous Cases?

The first thing that I noticed in this picture, by Liceti, were the exaggerated facial features, missing eyes and nakedness. I think most of us can agree that the folks in this picture are naked and weird. They are not admirably unique, rather they are smh weird.

Every office has those people, that no matter how hard you try, you just cannot figure out.

Who knows what planet they are from.

Don't try to figure it out, just color. It feels better.

Color it out...

FYI – this is another one for Find the Penis! Make it a competition! Have Fun!

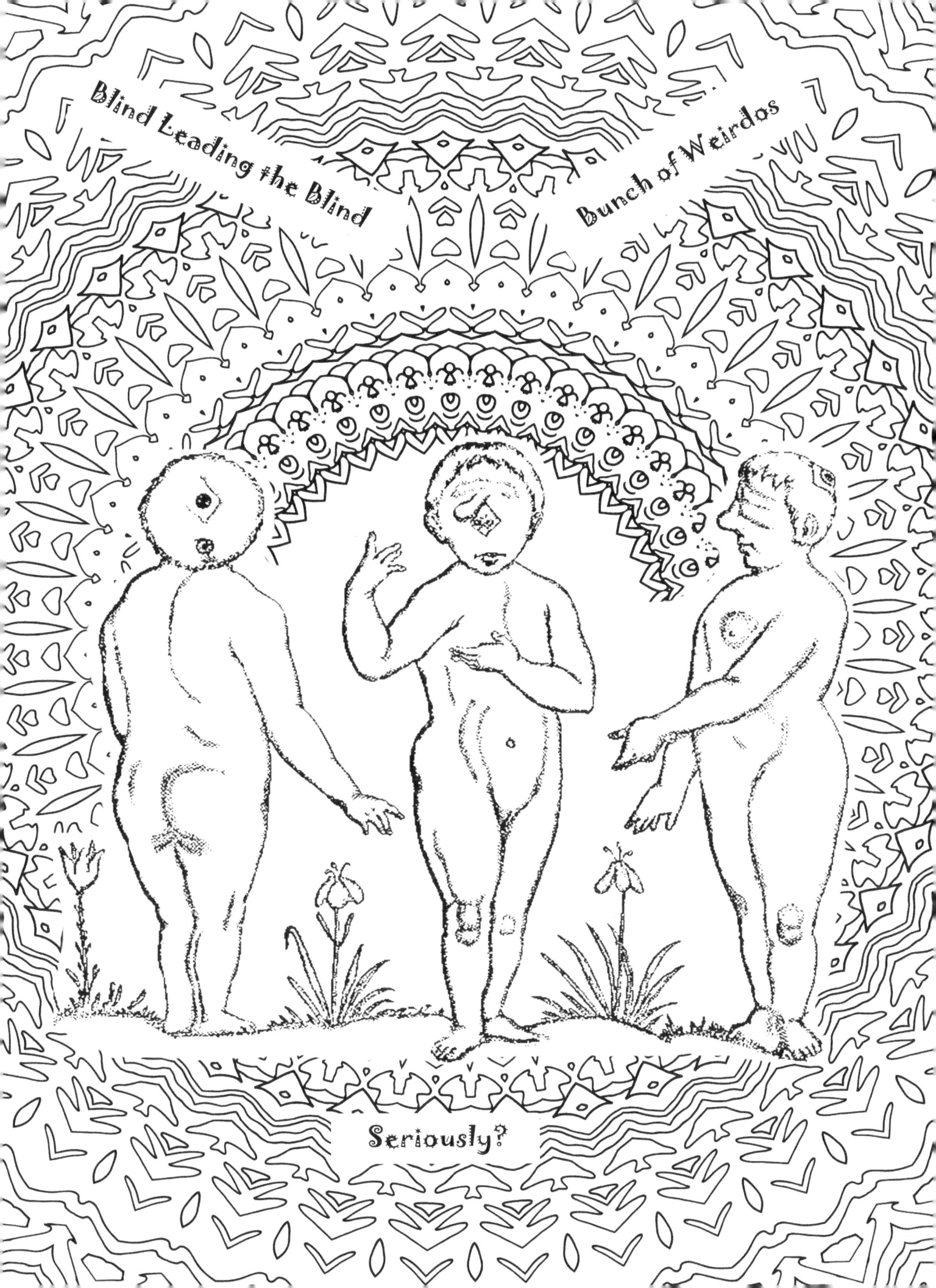

Sara -Hebi

さら蛇

Sara-Hebi is a large snake with the head of a woman. The folk-lore around this spirit is obscure, but let's just go with the ideas of deception, conspiracy, and untrustworthy behavior amongst co-workers. If at one time, in your working experience, you were wide-eyed and bushy-tailed, the fact that you have this coloring book means that it is safe to bet that you are not naive anymore.

Praise yourself for lessons learned and personal progress.

Color it out....

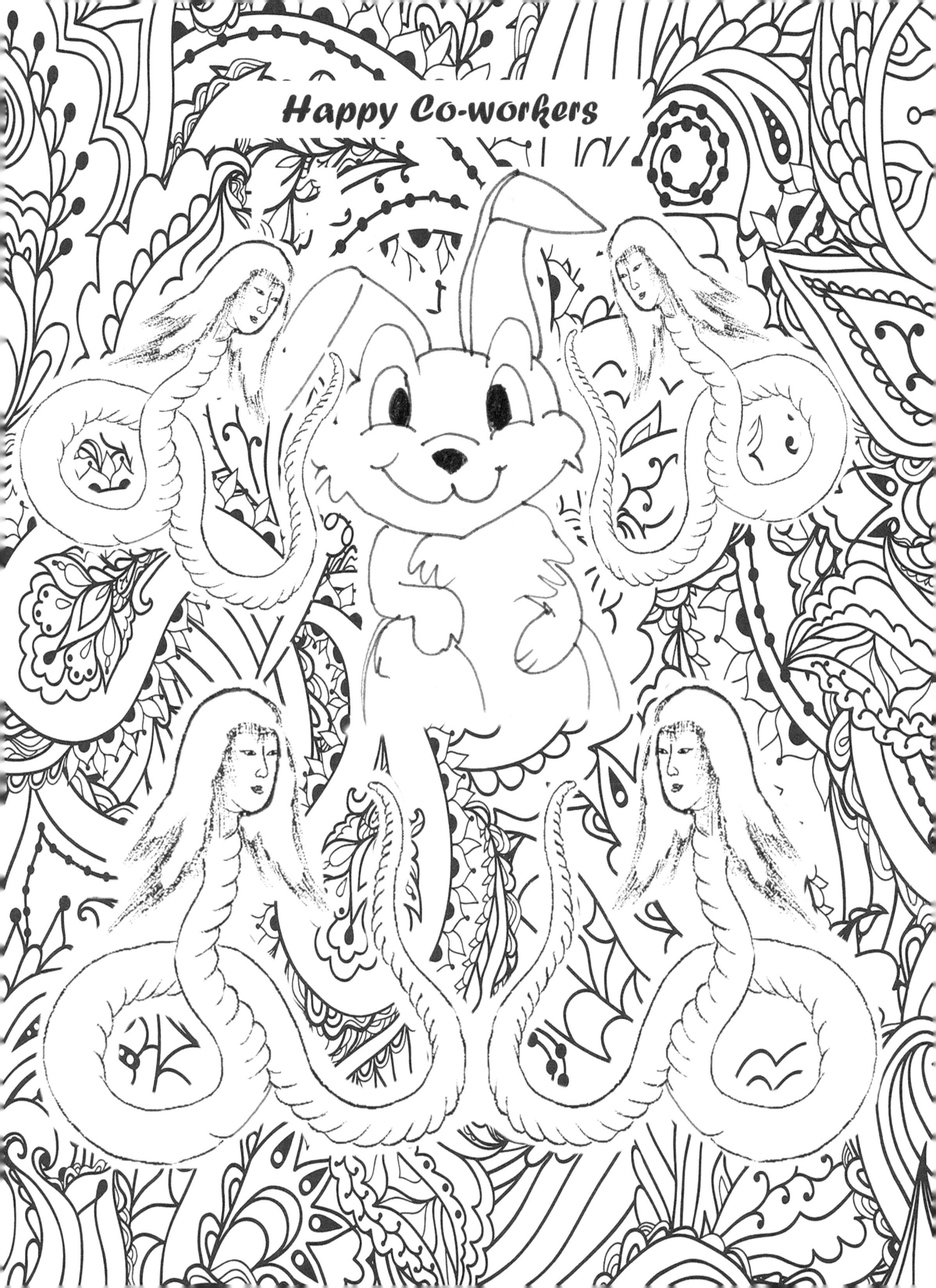

Happy Co-workers

Uwan

うわん

Uwan is named for the sound that the monster makes. He/she dwells in abandoned buildings and lives off of the fear that it causes.

I am sure that many of us can think of a co-worker or a task whose presence clears a room.

There is a blank line in the picture so that you can fill it with the name of whoever or whatever is scary and overwhelming. For some of us Uwan is definitely a person, (be careful adding in names of real people), but for others, it could just as easily be an activity like "fiscal reports" or "grant writing season".

Let your imagination flow.

Color it out....

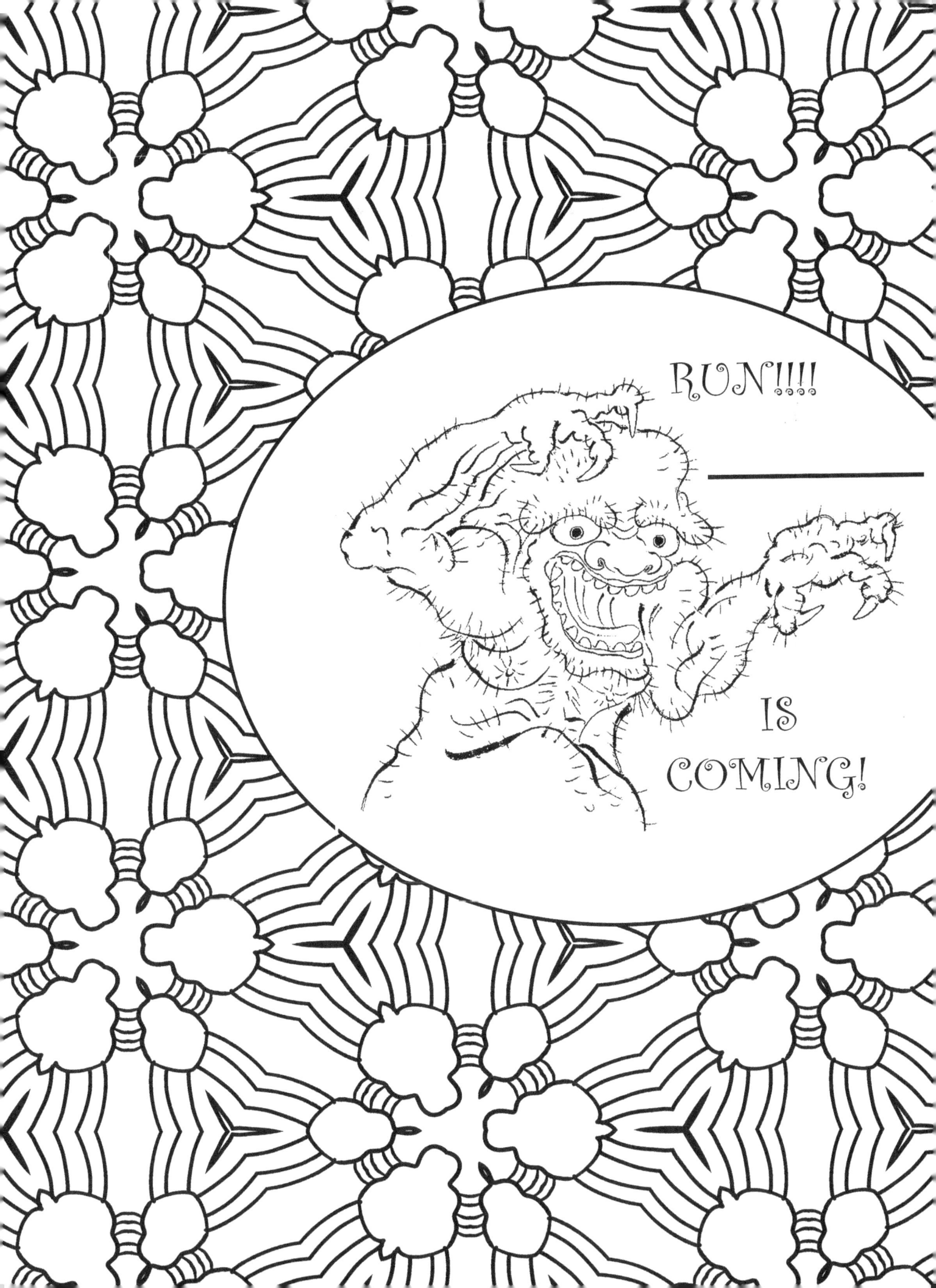

Byobu nozoki

屏風闚

Byōbu nozoki is a folding screen peeper. This spirit comes out of decorative folding screens or room dividers and leers at the people behind them when they are having sex.

Hopefully, you spend more nights unknowingly giving Byobu Nozoki a damned good show then you do with boring stuff from work.

If not, then my sincere hope for you is that change is coming.

Color it out...

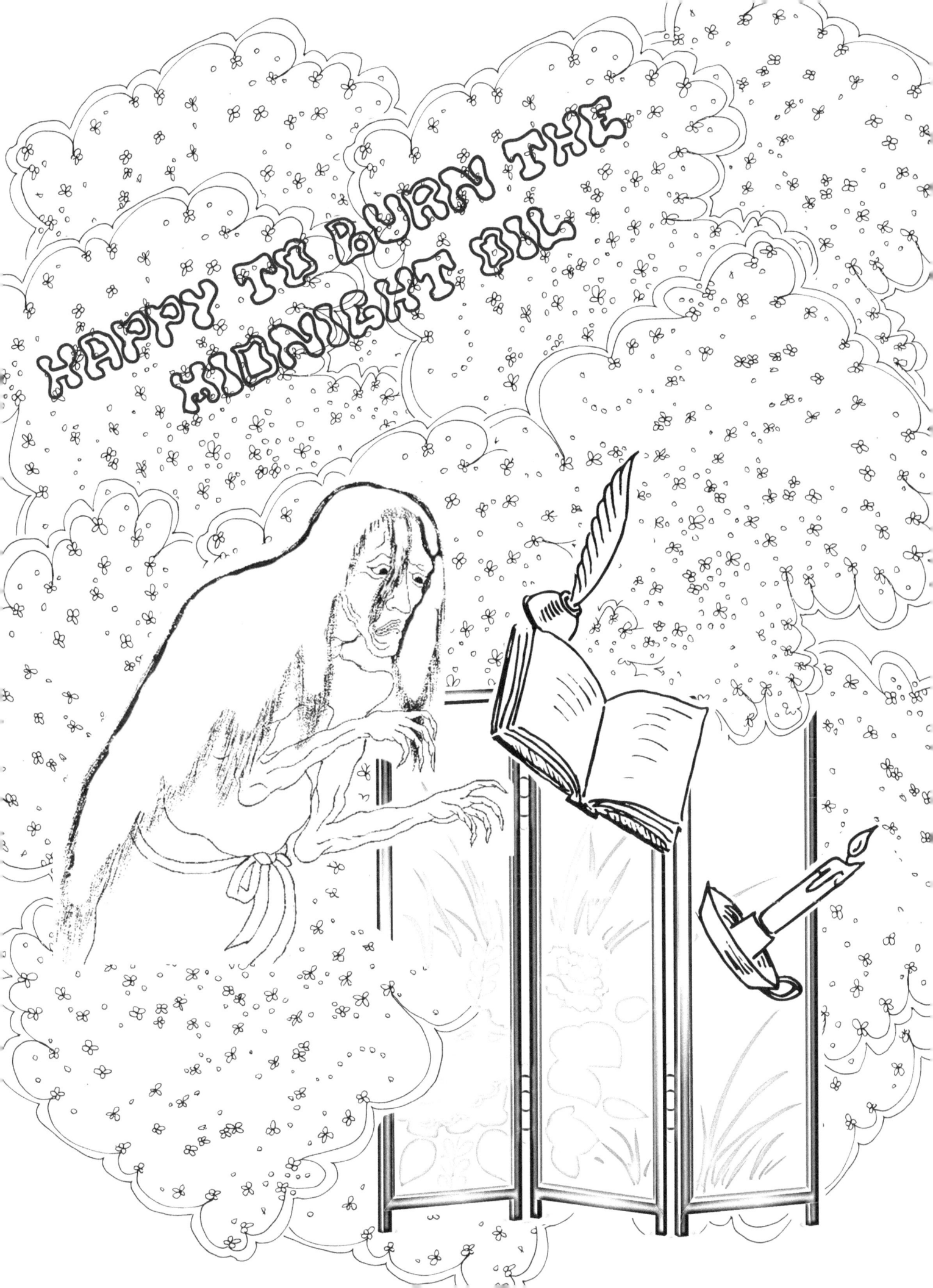

Odoroshi

おどろし

Odoroshi are wild creatures covered in a thick, unruly mane of hair. These masters of disguise are only seen when they want to be seen.

Don't you wish you could disappear when stressful deadlines are approaching?

Color it out...

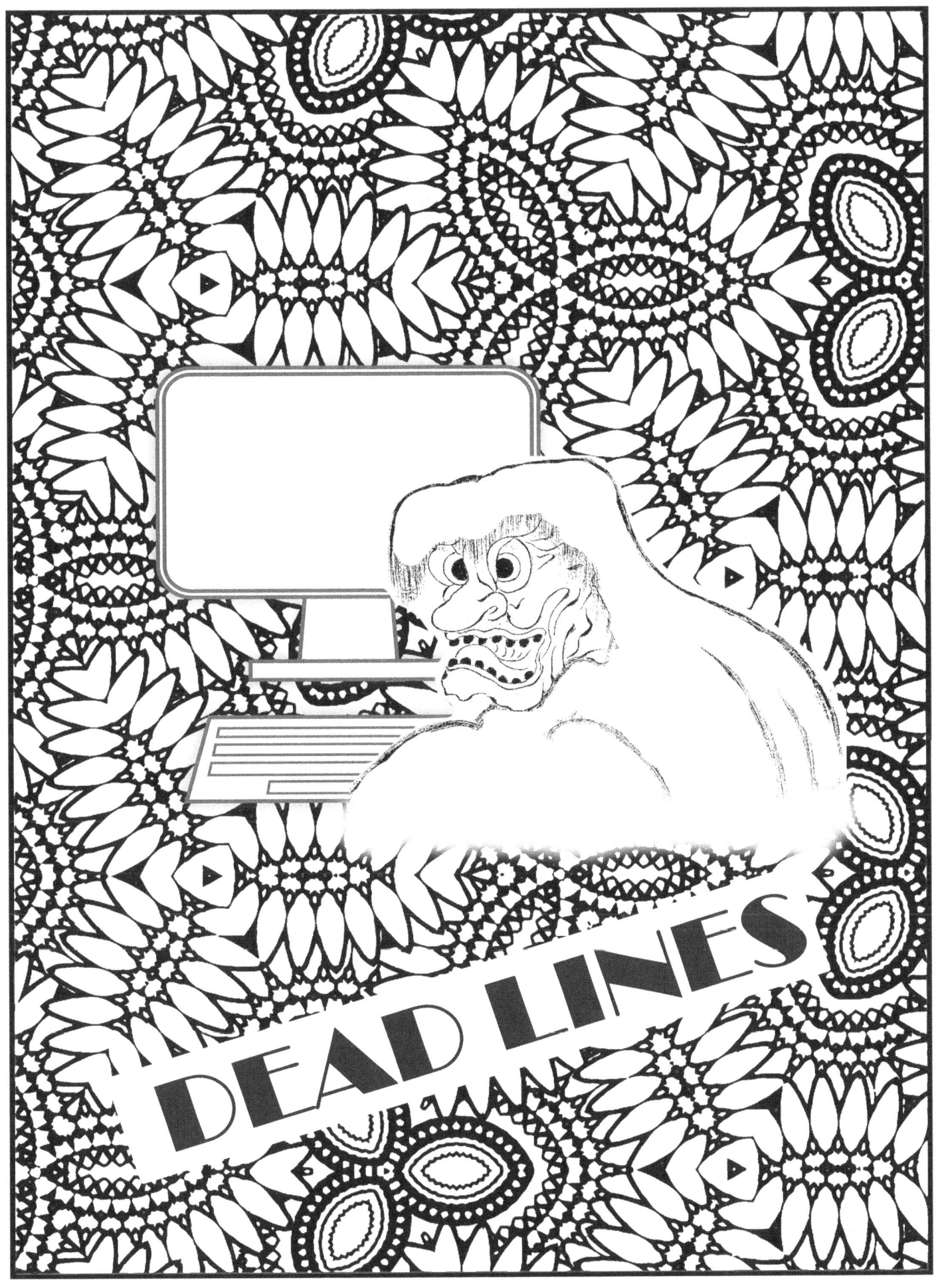

Kamikiri

髪切

Kamikiri are hair cutters who hang out in dark alleys, bathrooms, bedrooms and urban areas. They are known for sneaking up on people at night and unexpectedly cutting off their hair.

I immediately thought of people in service industries who are worn out from poor treatment by their clients/students/patients, etc.

There have definitely been times when the people I was supposed to be helping got on my last nerve. Often, I made ugly faces or pretended to kick these people when their backs were turned.

Compassion and customer Service Fatigue are real. If you are feeling disenchanted with the people you serve, let it go, remember to smile at work and

Color it out...

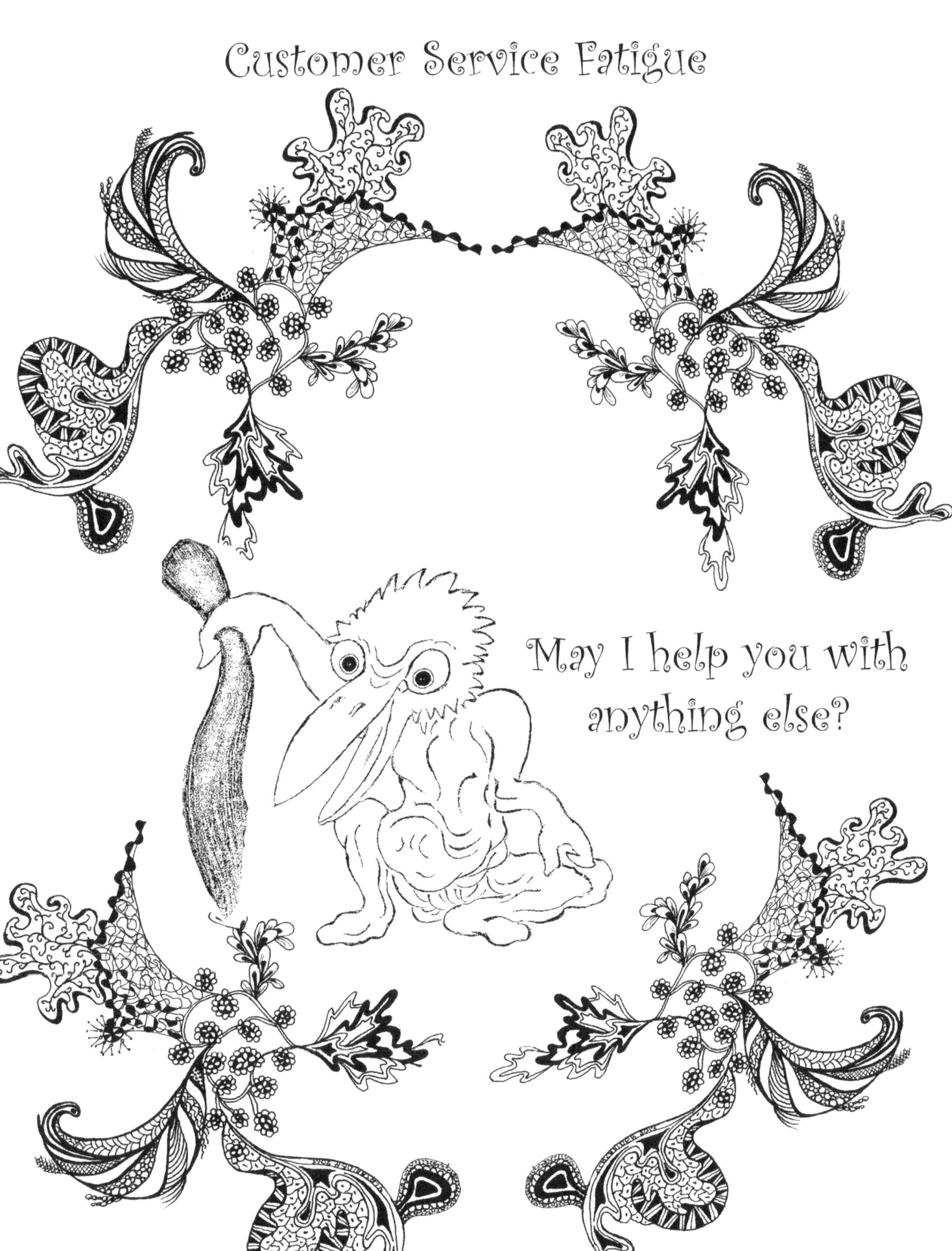

Customer Service Fatigue

May I help you with anything else?

Vrouw en Mannelijk Monster Met Kan en Beker

Woman and Male Monster with Can and Cup

This picture, by Arent van Bolten, made me think of office meetings.

As a teacher, staff meetings were usually a complete circus. Actually, it probably would have been a better use of time to stand on a desk and literally fart on everyone.

At least that would have been shockingly funny.

Color it out...

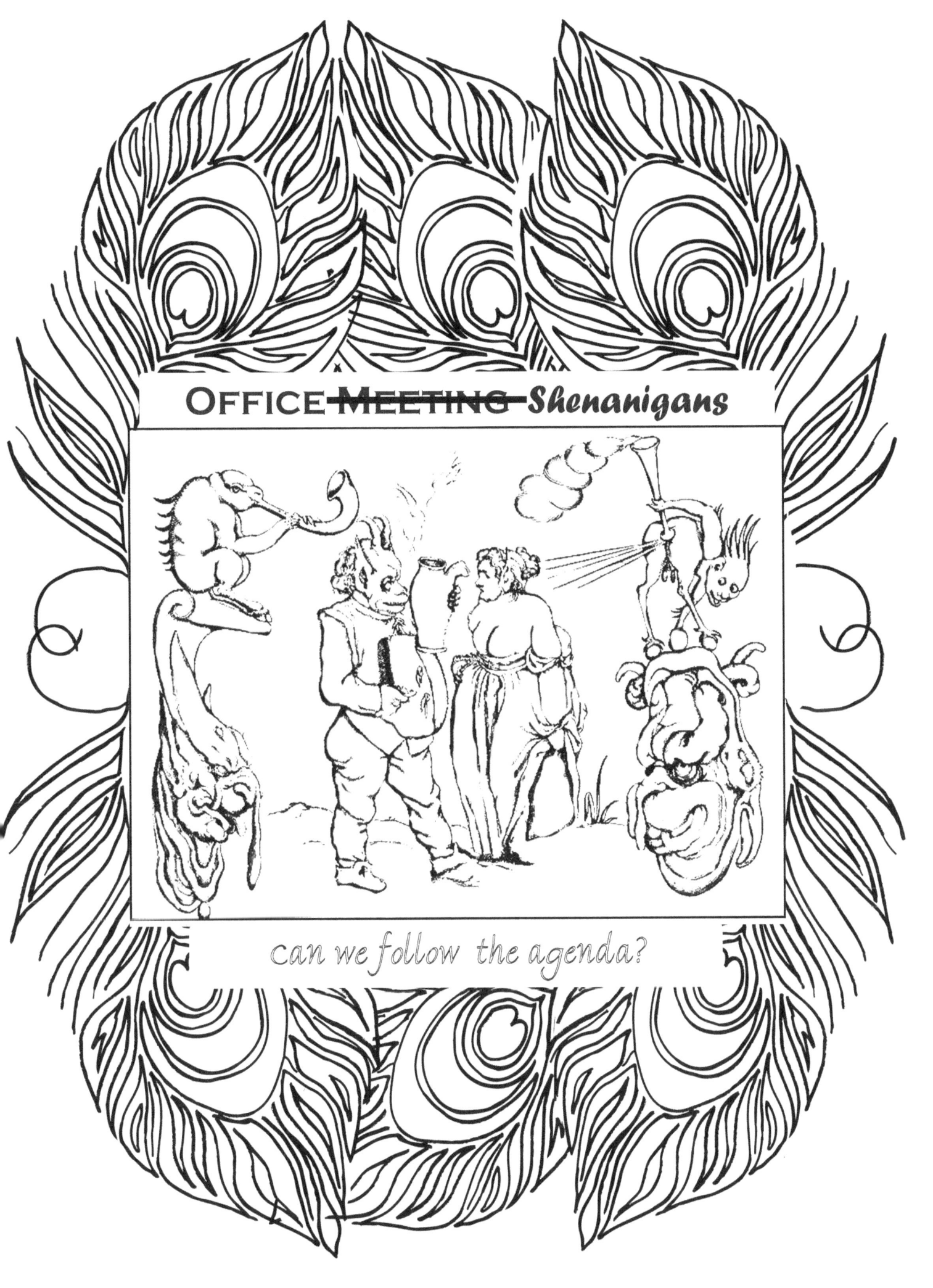

Ushi oni

牛鬼

Ushi oni is an ox demon, with the head of an ox and the body of a spider.

Ushi oni are cruel beasts who breath toxic poison and like to eat humans.

There were times at work when I felt like an Ushi oni surrounded by happy little butterflies waiting to be devoured.

Fortunately, I kept my hands to myself.

If you are feeling Ushi oni, you probably need therapy. If you try to make a counseling appointment, you will probably need more therapy because of the frustration involved in the process of getting an appointment.

Sooo, in the meantime, breathe and

Color it out...

You know it has been a good day if you didn't hit or bite anyone.

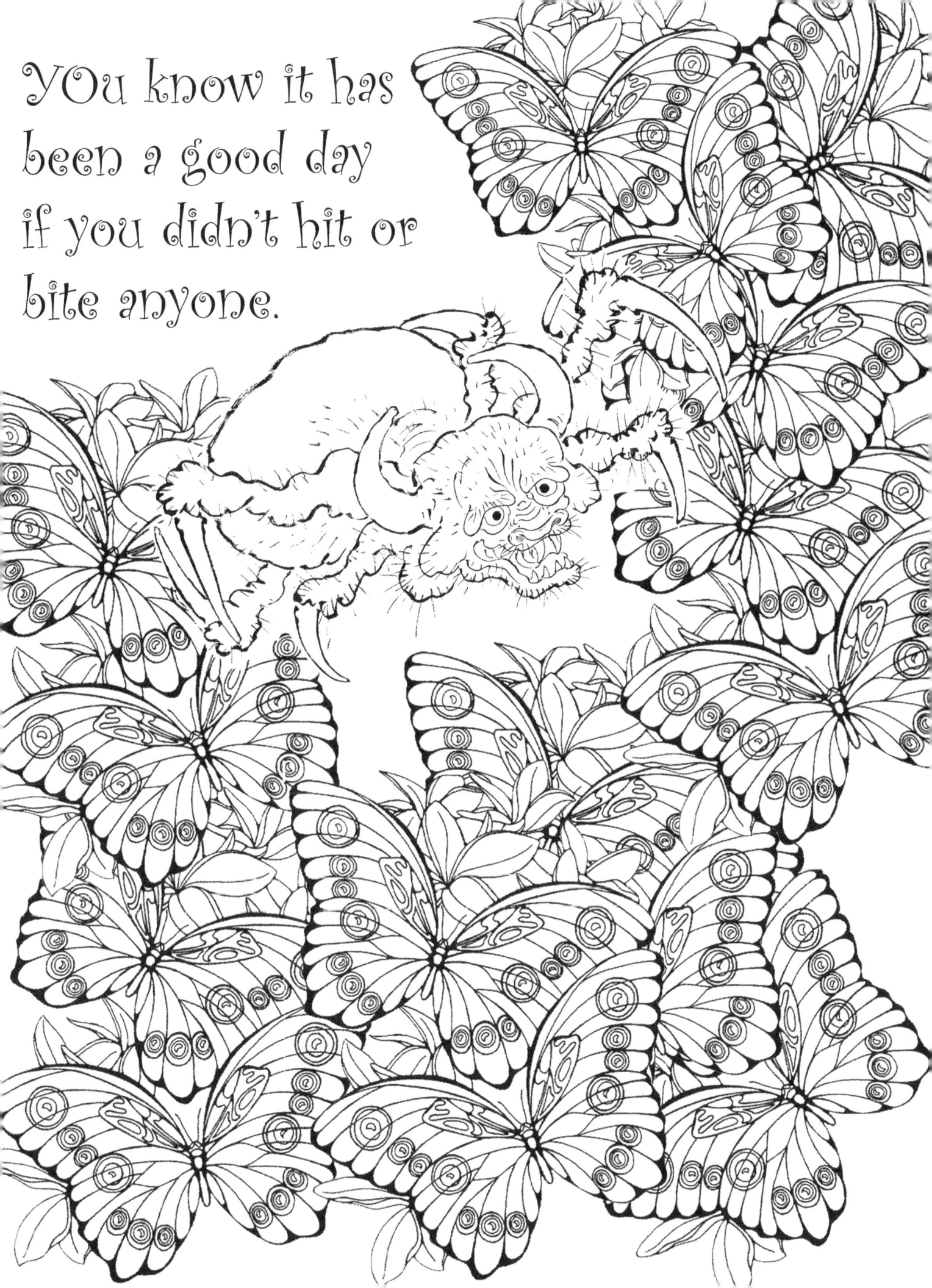

Daichiuchi

大地打

Daichiuchi means hammer priest. Some suggest that this Yokai is a spirit of cowardice associated with the proverb "to strike a stone bridge before crossing" (meaning to be excessively careful before doing anything).

Daichiuchi reminds me of the love/hate relationship that many of us have with work.

When you are feeling frustrated, instead of putting your fist through your computer screen, copy machine, or presentation,

Color it out...

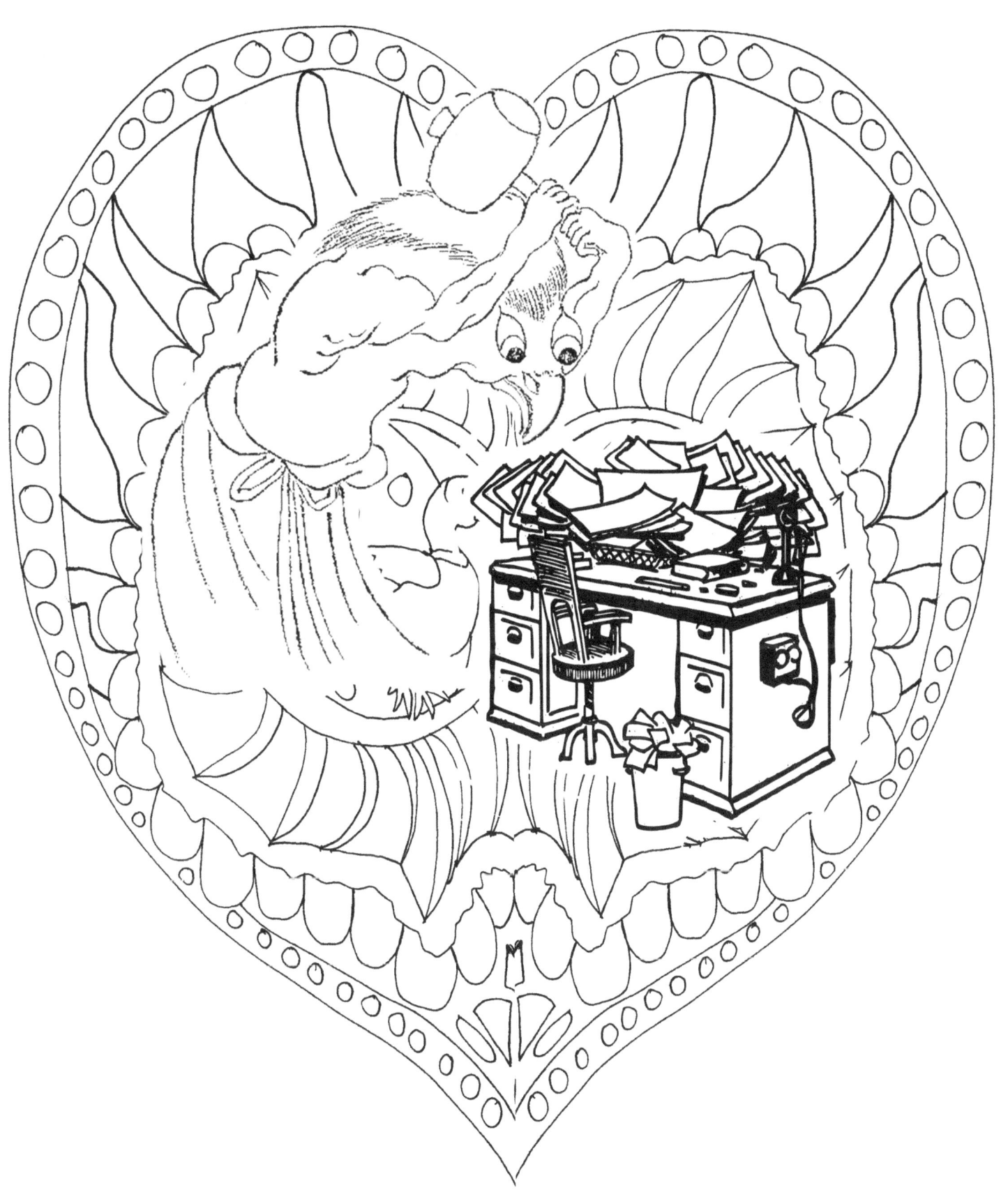

Yamawaro

山童

Yamawaro means mountain child. These Yokai are nature spirits who, when properly thanked, are known to help woodcutters
with their work.

As we work, many of us longingly wish for some improvement
in our circumstances.

If you don't want to dance for your hopes and dreams at least
color a picture.

Color it out...

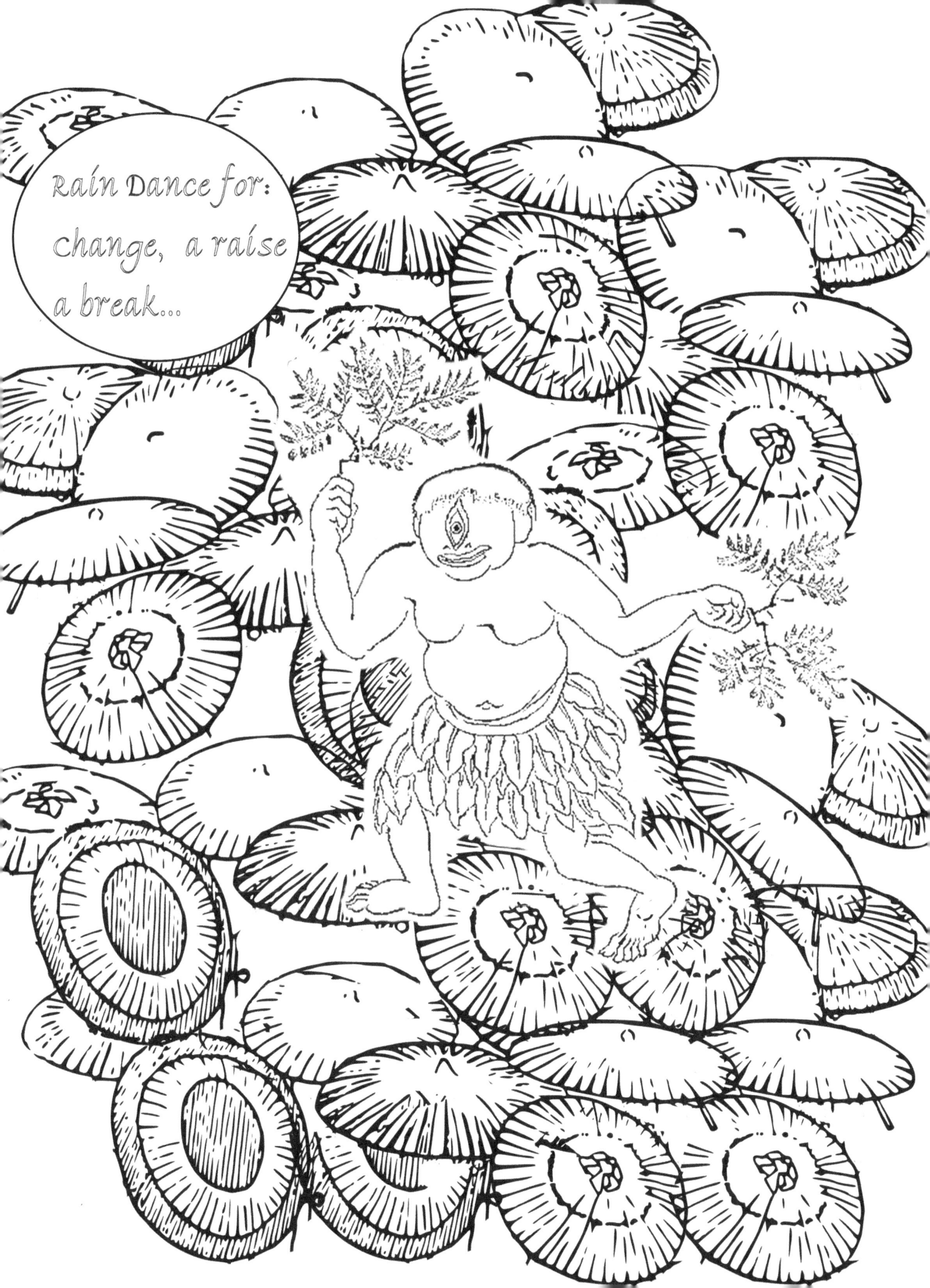

About the Author

I guess I should tell you about work experiences that might have inspired this book but, I feel like the pages of the book speak for themselves. Instead, I will tell you how I started to color.

I actually started coloring as an outlet for grief. My oldest child died tragically when he was 19 years old. Finding ways to release the pain of that loss was difficult. One thing that worked to decrease the intensity of the pain, was to "zone out" by listening to fantasy stories on audio books while coloring.

The process of coloring was slow and without pressure. I didn't have to explain, face people, or find words for emotions that have no names. I didn't have to think about the past, the future, or anything except the color and texture that I wanted to see in a spot on a page. I found that there was something about the process of creating, within the bounds of a pre-drawn image, that brought emotional relief.

So, how did my grief process turn into a coloring book about work?

For me, grief included a lot of "emotions" including, rage, impatience, authenticity, clarity of vision, a dark sense of humor, and a very low tolerance for bullshit. So how does one return to work with all of that churning through your veins? I have no idea. I am an entrepreneur now. When you figure it out, stop by the facebook page and let me know. In the meantime, laugh a wicked laugh, and color it out.

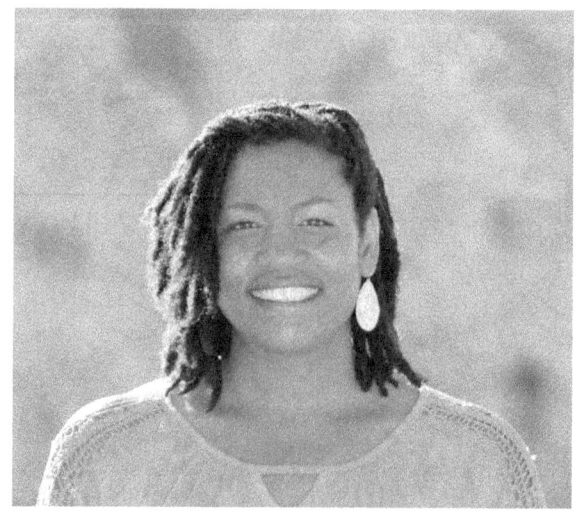

Did You Enjoy This Book?

WRITE A REVIEW

If you enjoyed this book, I would really appreciate it if you could take a minute to leave a review on Amazon at https://www.amazon.com/Monstrous-Office-Politics. Your review will help other people know that this book will lift their spirits and make the day more tolerable!

VISIT THE FACEBOOK PAGE

Please keep in touch! Visit the Monstrous Office Politics Facebook Page at https://www.facebook.com/Monstrousofficepolitics. Please like the page and share your coloring! Tell us funny stories and join in the fun around Office Politics!

GET UPDATES

Visit the MOP (Monstrous Office Politics) website at

https://nicolemarie1.wixsite.com/monstrous

and enter your name and email address. When I come out with a new book I will let you know! Please keep in touch...

And no matter what happens....

COLOR IT OUT!